THE KING OF WINGS

An Italian-American Chef's Journey to Culinary Fame

Written By

Bruno Pascale

Published by Franklin Publishers

Printed in the United States of America

For permissions, inquiries, or additional copies, contact:

Franklin Publishers

www.franklinpublishers.com

FRANKLIN PUBLISHERS

Dedication

This book, this journey—none of it would have been possible without the people who had my back through it all.

To my wife, Laurie A. Marinaro Pascale—my rock, my partner, the one who's stood by me through every late night, crazy idea, and big move. To my brother, Frank Pascale, for always being there, whether it was to give advice, call me out, or just support me when I needed it most.

To my daughters, Ava and Sophie, you're my world. Everything I do, every hustle, every grind—it's all for you.

To my team at Marley's, past and present—you guys are family. You put in the work, you make it happen, and Marley's wouldn't be what it is without you.

To my friends and supporters, the ones who showed up, ordered the food, spread the word, and believed in what I was building—you have no idea how much that means.

To all my instructors at the Hudson County Culinary Arts Institute—thank you for the knowledge, mentorship, and discipline that made me the chef I am today. In memory of Chef Paul Dillon.

And to my business partner, Joann Donaldson, for sticking with me, believing in me, and helping bring Marley's to life. Also to Jessica Westgate the "Chaos Coordinator" —for managing the madness every day and still showing up with a smile.

This book is for all of you.

Just Wing It.

Chef Bruno

Table of Contents

Introduction

You ever just know? Like deep in your gut, no doubt about it, this is what you were meant to do?

For me, that moment hit when I was just a kid—thirteen years old, standing in my family's kitchen in Newark, New Jersey, staring at the Pillsbury Doughboy on TV. Something about that little guy in his white chef's outfit stuck with me. I wanted to be him. I wanted the hat, the jacket, the whole thing. More than that, I wanted to cook. I didn't know it yet, but that one silly commercial set me on a path that would shape the rest of my life.

Now, I wasn't born into a restaurant empire. There was no family business waiting for me to inherit, no silver spoon, no safety net. I grew up in a big Italian family where food was everything—but making it a career? That was up to me. In a neighborhood like Newark, you didn't just sit around dreaming. You got to work.

First job? Busboy. Classic. Running plates, wiping down tables, peeking into the kitchen every chance I got. I was mesmerized. The heat, the flames, the controlled chaos of a working kitchen—it called to me. I watched the chefs work their magic, flipping pans, stretching dough, moving with a rhythm like music. That was where I belonged.

By seventeen, I was supposed to open a pizzeria with my father. He was going to help me get started, show me the ropes but life doesn't always follow the script. He passed away before we could make it happen. That changed everything. I left school, got my GED, and threw myself into the grind. Seven days a week, no breaks, no vacations—just long shifts in the kitchen, learning everything I could. If I was going to make it, I had to earn it the hard way.

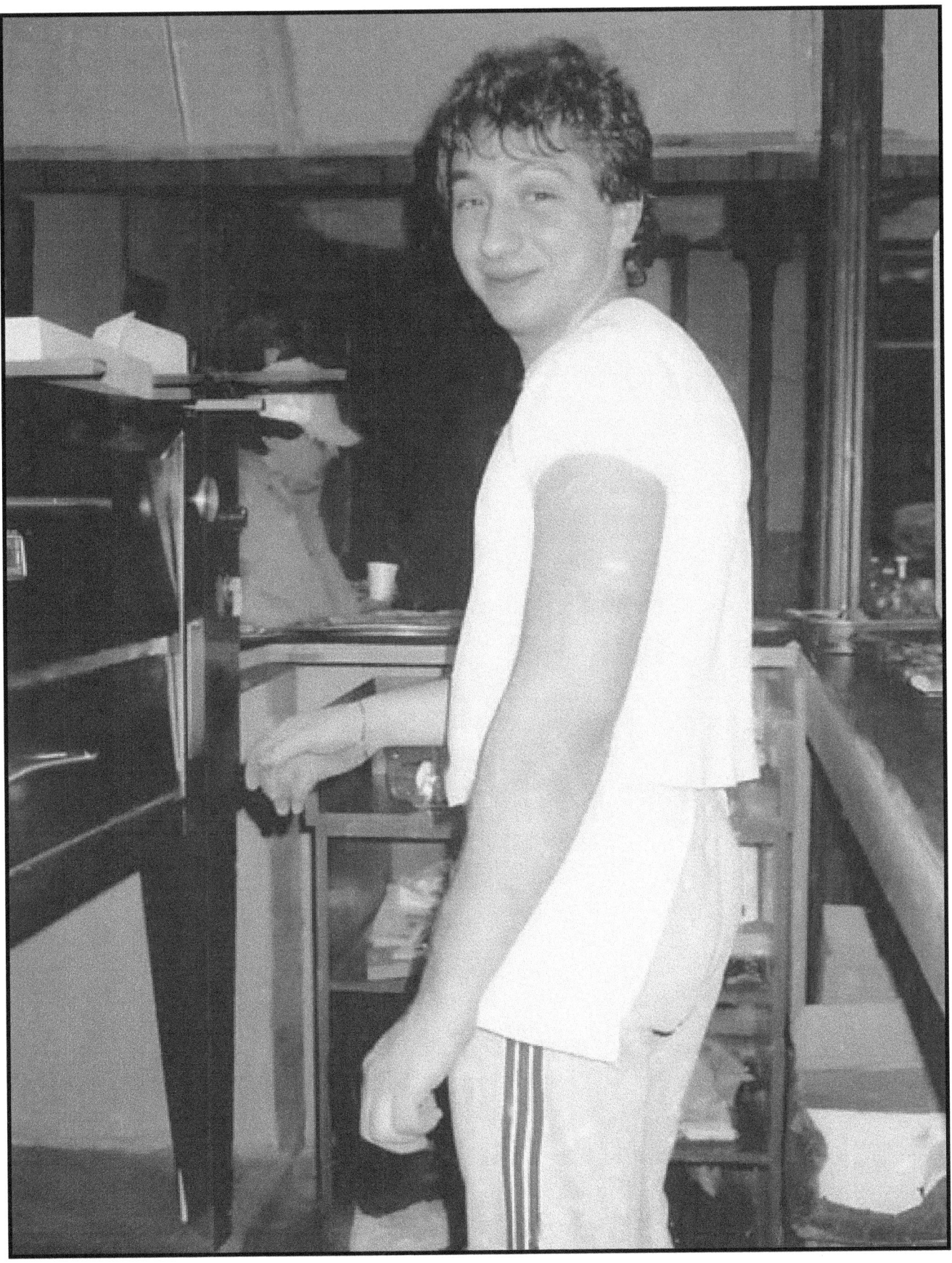

Bruno Pascale

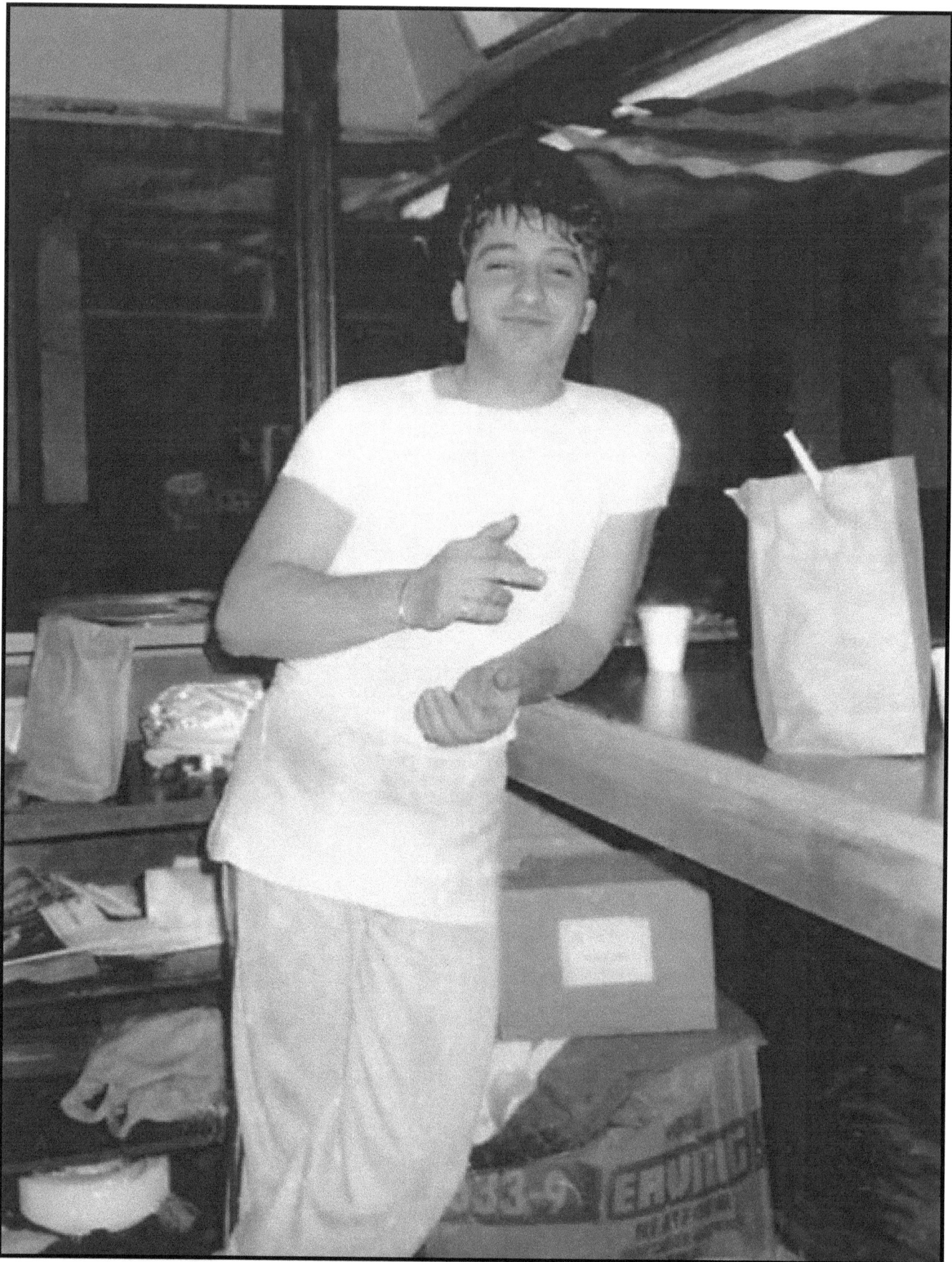

By seventeen, I got my first real taste of the pizzeria business as a partner but by eighteen, I did what most people my age couldn't even dream of—I opened my own pizzeria. My first place. Now, let me tell you, it wasn't some fancy grand opening. I wasn't a rich kid with a safety net. I had $1,500 to my name, and that was it. When I found out about a pizzeria for sale in Montclair, the guy wanted $11,000 for it. I looked him in the eye and said, "I'll give you what I got, and I'll work my ass off to pay the rest." He must've seen something in me because we shook on it. $225 a month in payments, and just like that—I owned my first pizzeria.

That was just the beginning. One restaurant turned into two. Two turned into five. Over the years, I opened more spots than I can count—cafés, pizzerias, Italian joints. I learned how to hustle, how to adapt, how to turn an idea into something real but no matter how many places I opened, there was always something in the back of my mind. A voice telling me I wasn't done yet. That I hadn't really left my mark

Then came the wings.

Now, if you'd asked me back then if I'd ever be known for chicken wings, I probably would've laughed in your face. I was an Italian chef. Pizza, pasta, risotto—that's what I did but when I opened Marley's Gotham Grill, I had an idea. What if I made it the go-to spot for wings? Not just any wings—hundreds of flavors. Wings people couldn't get anywhere else.

I started experimenting. Peanut butter, habanero, and jelly wings. Crab meat Pizza. Philly cheesesteak Pizza. People thought I was crazy. Maybe I was but you know what? It worked.

Fast forward a few years, and I wasn't just making wings—I was redefining them. I went from a guy with a dream to The King of Wings, with over 350 different flavors and counting. People drove in from all over just to try them. I started winning competitions breaking records, and before I knew it, I was standing in front of cameras on the Food Network, competing against some of the best chefs in the world. I walked in as the underdog and walked out a champion.

Looking back, it's crazy to think about how it all started. A kid with a dream, a busboy wiping down tables, a guy scraping together every dollar he had just to keep his doors open. Now? Now, I get to share my story with you. The highs, the lows, the hustle, the grind, and of course—the wings.

Because if there's one thing I've learned in this wild journey, it's this: life, like cooking, isn't about following a perfect recipe. It's about taking risks, mixing unexpected ingredients, and sometimes—just winging it.

CHAPTER 1

The Hustle Begins

They say the kitchen is the heart of the home, but for me, it was the heart of my entire world. From the moment I took that first job as a busboy, I knew I wasn't just working—I was learning. Every plate I cleared, every table I wiped, I was watching, absorbing, figuring out what made a restaurant run and let me tell you, it wasn't just about the food. It was about the energy, the movement, the rhythm of a kitchen in full swing.

I was just a teenager in Newark, New Jersey, hungry—literally and figuratively—to make something of myself. When my father passed away, my whole world shifted. We were supposed to open a pizzeria together, but life had other plans. It was up to me to take what he taught me and make it happen on my own. I had two choices: give up or double down and giving up was never in my DNA.

So, I went all in. Seven days a week, long shifts, no vacations, no breaks. I lived in that kitchen, learning from every chef I met, picking up techniques, watching how they moved, how they thought, how they made food come to life but here's the thing—being a great chef isn't just about cooking. It's about understanding the business, the grind, the numbers. You can make the best food in the world, but if you can't run a business, you won't last.

Learning the Business

That's when I knew I had to do more than just work—I had to educate myself. So, in 1985, at around 20 years old, I enrolled in the Culinary Arts Institute in Jersey City. I was balancing school and work, pushing myself harder than ever before but life had another curveball waiting for me—I became a father, and just like that, my priorities shifted again. I had a son to provide for, and school had to take a back seat. I took a break, put my head down, and focused on work. The goal never changed—I was going to make something of myself. It just had to happen on a different timeline.

After a few years of grinding, I knew I had to go back and finish what I started. So I returned to Culinary school and didn't just graduate—I graduated summa cum laude. I won the Salute to Excellence Award, which sent me to Chicago to meet some of the biggest names in the culinary world. That moment, standing among the best, proved to me that I wasn't just some kid with a dream—I was on my way to becoming a force in this industry.

But degrees and awards don't pay the bills. I needed to open more restaurants, build something bigger, take everything I had learned, and put it into action. I opened The Laughing Lion with my brother Frank in 1991 in Dover, New Jersey—our first real Italian restaurant. We poured our hearts into it, and it became the foundation for everything that came next. Over the years, I built a culinary empire—Café Z at Rutgers University, Mad City Café and Grill in North Brunswick, Ristorante Il Porto in Sparta, Shaker Café, Mad Chef Café in Flemington, Goodfellas Pizzeria in Ringos, and, of course, Marley's in Hackettstown, which would eventually become the home of the wings that made me famous.

The Birth of a Culinary Empire

But before I ever became the King of Wings, I was just a guy hustling to keep my restaurants alive. Running a restaurant isn't glamorous—it's a war zone. You've got to be fast, adaptable, and ready to handle anything. One broken freezer can cost you thousands. One bad review can kill your reputation. One slow season can put you out of business, and yet, I kept pushing, kept taking risks, kept finding ways to stand out.

That's where the creativity started to come in. I wasn't interested in making the same dishes as everyone else. If I was going to make a name for myself, I had to do things differently, and that's where the wings started creeping into my menu. First, it was just a few flavors—nothing crazy but then I started thinking bigger. Why settle for ten flavors when I could make fifty? A hundred? Three hundred? No one was doing that. No one even thought it was possible.

At first, people thought I was nuts. Peanut butter and jelly wings? Crab meat Pizza? Cheesesteak Pizza? But once they tried them, they got it. It wasn't about making something weird—it was about making something unforgettable.

Taking Wings to the Next Level

But the journey didn't stop there. It was one thing to make unique wings another to put them on the map. That's when the competitions started. I wanted to prove that I wasn't just playing around—I was serious about this. I entered every contest I could, traveling all over to show people that wings weren't just a bar snack—they could be an art form.

One of my biggest moments was stepping onto the stage of the Food Network. That was my bucket list moment, something I had dreamed about since I started. Competing against some of the best chefs in the world, I didn't just hold my own—I won, and when I walked off that stage, I knew this wasn't just about wings anymore. It was about proving that I had built something real, something that would last.

The Roots That Built Me

And through all of this, my roots kept me grounded. My parents, my family, the traditions they passed down to me—they shaped me into the chef and businessman I became. My father's love for fresh ingredients, my mother's dedication to making meals from scratch, the way they would gather everyone around the table on Sundays and holidays—those moments built my palate, my work ethic, my love for food.

I still remember those long days when my mother would be outside, boiling marinara sauce in massive vats over an open fire, canning it to last through the winter. Those flavors, those smells—they stuck with me, and they became part of everything I created in the kitchen. The traditions of my Italian heritage and the hustle of an American entrepreneur combined to create something entirely my own.

And it wasn't just about food. It was about legacy. It was about pushing boundaries, doing what no one else was willing to try. My heritage wasn't just in the ingredients—it was in the way I built my business, the way I hustled, the way I never took no for an answer.

This chapter of my life was all about the grind. The late nights. The early mornings. The risks. The failures. The wins. The lessons learned the hard way. I wasn't just cooking—I was building, and every dish, every mistake, every crazy idea was leading me to what would eventually become my legacy.

I wasn't just making food. I was making history.

CHAPTER 2

Breaking 100 – The Flavor Revolution

It started as a gimmick. Just something fun to bring people into the restaurant, to shake things up. At that time, I had no idea I was about to change the game completely. I had opened my place, Marley's, in 2009, and like any restaurant owner, I wanted to get people talking. I figured, why not make it a competition? I'd seen those hot-wing challenges where people signed liability waivers before torching their taste buds, but I wasn't interested in making people suffer. I wanted something different.

So I thought, let's do a simple wing-eating contest. Whoever eats the most wings in a sitting gets a free meal, a T-shirt, and their picture on the wall. It was the kind of idea that could go either way—be a total flop or become a local sensation.

Turns out people loved it.

The First 100

The first guy to take on the challenge polished off 40 wings in one sitting. The next guy, trying to outdo him, hit 55 wings in one night. Week after week, customers came in, trying to beat the record. The energy was electric. People came in not just to eat but to be part of something but I quickly realized something: this wasn't about just stuffing your face—it was about the wings themselves.

That's when it hit me. Why stop at just a few flavors? Why not push the boundaries of what people expected from wings?

At that time, most places had maybe a dozen flavors—Buffalo, BBQ, Garlic Parmesan if they were feeling fancy but I wanted Marley's to be different. I wanted to be the guy nobody could catch. So I started experimenting. I set an initial goal: 101 wing flavors. No other restaurant in New Jersey had that. Not even the big chains. If I could get there, I'd be untouchable.

I started out with the classics—Buffalo, Honey BBQ, Garlic Parmesan but those weren't going to get me to 101. I had to get creative. That's when the real magic started happening in my kitchen.

I was in the back, mixing sauces like a mad scientist, throwing different combinations together. Some were good, some were disasters, and some were so weird that even I hesitated before tasting them but that's how the legends were born.

The Night It Happened

One night, I was standing over the fryer, tossing a fresh batch of wings, when my business partner at the time, Joann Donaldson, walked in. She was helping type up the new menu with all the flavors I'd been experimenting with.

She looked up from her notes and said, "Bruno, you wanted 101 flavors, right?" I nodded.

"Well, you're at 103."

I froze. 103? We overshot it?

I glanced at the list, and sure enough, I had passed my goal without even realizing it but instead of stopping, my brain went into overdrive.

"Then we're not stopping," I said.

That night, I knew we had something special.

Going Beyond 101

That was the moment that changed everything. The number 101 wasn't a goal anymore—it was just a stepping stone. Over the next year, we doubled it. Then we tripled it. Soon, we were over 200 flavors, then 250, then 400.

It became an obsession. Every time I thought I'd hit the peak, I'd come up with something crazier, more unexpected. Customers weren't just coming in to eat anymore—they were coming to see what new flavors I had on the menu. They were coming in to be surprised.

And the flavors? Oh, they were wild. Some became instant classics. Some had people scratching their heads until they tasted them but every single one had a story.

The Hall of Fame – The Wings That Made It Happen

Here's a list of the flavors that put Marley's on the map, the ones that made me realize there were no rules when it came to wings.

The Classics with a Twist

- Bang Bang – A flavor that became one of my personal favorites. Spicy, a little sweet, and packed with flavor.

- Sticky Crispy Garlic – A perfect balance of crunchy, garlicky, and a little sweet.

- Garlic Parmesan – One of the OG flavors, but the way we did it? Unbeatable.

The Wild Experiments That Worked

- Strawberry Mojito – One of my waitresses had been with me for 10 years. One day, she asked, "Can you name one after me?" She loved mojitos, so I made a strawberry mojito wing. Turned out to be a hit.

- Pop Your Cherry – Cherry liqueur sauce with maraschino cherries served with Pop Rocks on the side. You take a bite, and the candy pops in your mouth. Insane.

- Victoria's Secret Hot & Naughty – Inspired by one of my bartenders. Sweet heat with a serious kick.

- Naughty Barbie – Hot & Naughty, but with a BBQ twist. A favorite among the regulars.

- Jamaica Me Crazy – Jerk seasoning, a little vinegar, and just the right balance of heat.

The Dessert Wings (Yes, Dessert Wings)

- OMG Wing – Oreo cookie crumb, marshmallow, and chocolate ganache. Yep, on a wing.

- Elvis – Banana, peanut butter, and bacon. Because if it was good enough for Elvis, it was good enough for my menu.

- S'mores – Marshmallow, graham cracker, and chocolate sauce. Campfire vibes on a chicken wing.

- Nutella Chocolate with Bacon & Cashew Nuts – Just trust me on this one.

The Game-Changers

- Kung Fu (Bruce Lee's Favorite) – A honey ginger soy glaze that punches you right in the taste buds.

- Hawaiian BBQ – A tropical spin on a BBQ sauce that became a top-seller.

- Peach Whiskey – Fresh peaches, brown sugar, whiskey reduction. A little sweet, a little smoky, a little boozy.

- Raspberry Habanero – The perfect mix of sweet and deadly.

CHAPTER 3

The First Taste of Fame – Print Media Puts Me on the Map

After crossing the 100-wing flavor mark, something changed. It wasn't just a crazy idea anymore—it was something people were talking about. At first, it was just the customers. Word of mouth started spreading, and before I knew it, people were driving hours just to try the wings but the real moment that put me on the map wasn't a packed restaurant or a line out the door—it was when I saw my name in print.

I'll never forget it. Holding that first newspaper article in my hands, seeing my face and my restaurant in bold letters—it made everything real. It meant I wasn't just making wings—I was building something, and once the media got a taste? They couldn't get enough.

Pocono Wing–Off – The First Step Toward Fame

Everything started with the Pocono Wing-Off. This was the biggest wing competition in the area, held every year in the Poconos, Pennsylvania. It wasn't just a bunch of backyard cooks throwing some wings in a fryer—this was serious business.

The setup was brutal. Every competitor had to bring their own fryers, their own wings, their own sauces. If you weren't prepared, you were screwed. The event started early in the morning, and by noon, thousands of people were showing up. The crowd would taste-test wings from every booth and vote for their favorites in different categories:

- Best Wing
- Most Creative Wing

- Hottest Wing

I wasn't just there to compete—I was there to win, and I did.

In 2011, I won for Best Honey BBQ Wing. That was huge. Winning that title, beating out 25 to 30 other restaurants—it was my first taste of what it felt like to be recognized for what I could do.

The next year, 2012, I did it again—this time, taking home the title for Best Garlic Parmesan Wing. That win? It wasn't just another trophy. It was momentum. It was the start of people realizing that Marley's wasn't just another wing joint—this was something special.

And then came the rivalry.

At one of the competitions, there was this guy from Philly who called himself "The King of Wings." He had the signs, the branding, the attitude. He thought he had it in the bag but when the results came in and I took home the win, I walked up to him and said:

"You're the Queen of Wings now."

I wasn't trying to be mean—I was just letting him know there was a new king in town, and from that moment on, I knew: I wasn't just playing the game—I was changing it.

The Press Takes Notice

Winning at the Pocono Wing-Off didn't just get me bragging rights—it got me media attention. The first time I saw my name in print was in Lehigh Valley Live (2011), under a feature called Wing Showdown. Seeing my name in a real newspaper? That was a whole new level.

After that, it was like a chain reaction. Once one publication ran a story, everyone else wanted in.

- Daily Record (2014) – "140 Varieties of Wings"
  - This was the first article that made people realize just how deep my obsession went. Up until then, most people thought, "Okay, this guy makes some wings." But 140 flavors? That's when they knew—this guy's not normal.

- Star-Ledger (2014) – "Winging It"
  - This one really gave me some credibility. The Star-Ledger wasn't some small-town paper—this was big time in New Jersey. They painted me as this mad scientist of wings, a guy who wasn't afraid to push the boundaries of what a wing could be.

- NJ.com (2017) – "New Jersey's Best of the Best"
  - At this point, it wasn't just about having a unique wing shop—people were calling me the best, and not just in one town, not just in one county—in the whole damn state.

- Unflappable (August 11, 2014)
  - o This article focused on my dedication to the craft. They didn't just talk about my flavors—they talked about the process, the passion, the long hours. People started realizing that I wasn't just making wings—I was creating an experience.

- Express Times (2011) – Another early feature that helped spread my name.

Every time an article came out, business exploded. Suddenly, people were driving in from out of state just to try my wings. I was getting calls for interviews, invitations to events, and offers to collaborate with other restaurants.

It was surreal. I had gone from a kid with $1,500 to a guy making headlines.

Food Network & Munchmobile – The National Stage

Print media got me local fame but then, I got the big call.

Food Network.

I entered a competition and ended up winning $10,000. NJ.com covered it with the headline: "New Jersey Chef Wins $10,000 on Food Network."

That moment? It changed everything.

After that, the Star-Ledger's Munchmobile featured me, calling me a "wing genius." They sent out a food critic to try my wings, and his reaction? Mind-blown. That's when I realized: this isn't just a local thing anymore. People all over the country are paying attention.

The Moment It Sank In

I'll never forget the day I walked into the restaurant, and there was a line out the door before we even opened.

I asked a customer, "How'd you hear about us?"

He held up a newspaper and said, "This guy right here. I had to see if the hype was real."

That's when it hit me. This wasn't luck. This wasn't a fluke.

This was hard work paying off.

I had spent years perfecting my wings, experimenting, pushing limits, and now? People were talking. Newspapers were writing. Customers were coming from hours away just to get a taste.

And I wasn't even close to being done.

Lights, Camera, Wings — When TV Took Over

Print media got people talking. TV made them show up.

After the newspapers and magazines started rolling in, business exploded but nothing—and I mean nothing—compared to the power of being on live television.

When you're in print, people read about you. When you're on TV, they feel like they know you. They see your face, they hear your voice, and suddenly, you're not just a name in an article—you're a person they want to meet.

I didn't plan on being a TV personality. I was just a guy making crazy wings but when the cameras showed up, I leaned in. Because why not? I wasn't just going to be the best wing guy in New Jersey. I was going to be the most memorable.

New York Live — The Breakthrough Moment

It all started with a random conversation at a Pennsylvania gym.

Some bodybuilders were working out, talking about wings. They were saying:

"Once we're done here, we gotta go to Marley's. They got 300 flavors."

A producer for New York Live overheard them and thought, No way. That can't be real.

She called up Lauren Scala, one of the biggest names in New York media, and told her:

"You need to check this place out. This is a story."

Next thing I know, I get a call at the restaurant.

Lauren Scala and her crew wanted to come out—immediately.

There was no planning, no script, no time to overthink it. They were coming the next day to film.

Filming Day — No Scripts, Just Wings

When they walked in, I knew this was big time.

Lauren Scala wasn't just some random local reporter—she was a pro, and she had one job: find the best food spots and put them in front of the whole country.

She walked in, saw the menu, and said:

"You really have 300 flavors?"

I smiled and said, "You're about to try them."

I wasn't nervous. This was my arena. I had spent years perfecting my craft, so when the cameras rolled, I did what I always did:

- I cooked.

- I explained the flavors.

- I let Lauren taste every single one.

And here's the thing—she wasn't faking it. Every reaction was real. She tried 15 different wings, and she loved every single one.

Then, she asked me about the flavors, and I hit her with one of my favorites:

"This is the Bang Bang wing."

"This one's the Boom Boom wing."

She stopped and repeated:

"Bang Bang... Boom Boom?"

And in her classic New Yorker accent, it sounded hilarious.

It became an inside joke. She couldn't stop saying it. She was cracking up, the camera guys were laughing, and I knew—this is going to be good.

The Power of National TV

The segment aired before the Super Bowl.

Which means?

Millions of people saw it.

When it hit the screen, my phone started blowing up. Customers, friends, family—everybody saw it.

- People were tagging me on social media.

- My inbox was flooded with messages.

- The next day, lines wrapped around the building.

I had never seen anything like it.

Lauren Scala even told me, "I'll come back when you hit 350 flavors."

So what did I do?

I made 50 more flavors in two weeks.

I texted her:

"Lauren, I got 350 now. You coming back?"

She laughed and told me she was busy, but I knew she meant it—she'd be back.

News 12, Lehigh Valley, and More TV Appearances

After New York Live, TV stations started calling left and right.

One of the biggest early features was News 12 New Jersey.

They covered a voting competition we were in, where things got so competitive that eventually, they just let everyone win.

We also had coverage from:

- Lehigh Valley News

- Express Times (2011) – The first print & video coverage of my wings

- News 4 Live New York – Another huge moment

- WFMZ – Covered a charity event we did with food trucks

At this point, I had been featured in:

- TV segments

- Online video reports

- National and local newspapers

People knew my name.

The Food Network Win – $10,000 in the Bag

I had competed in local contests before. I had gone up against chefs who thought they were the best and proved them wrong.

But competing on Food Network? That was another level.

I went in knowing one thing:

"They're about to see what I can really do."

And I won.

Not just any win—$10,000.

NJ.com covered it with the headline:

"New Jersey Chef Wins $10,000 on Food Network."

After that, it was like everything went into overdrive.

- More TV appearances.

- More interviews.

- More customers coming from all over the country.

This wasn't just a local success story anymore.

This was nationwide.

Seeing Myself on TV – The Moment It Hit Me

The day after my New York Live segment aired, I walked into the restaurant.

And there it was.

A line out the door.

People weren't just coming for the wings. They were coming because they had seen me on TV. They knew my face, my story, my flavors.

One guy walked in, holding his phone up, playing the clip of Lauren Scala saying "Bang Bang, Boom Boom."

He pointed at the screen and said:

"I had to try it. Is it really that good?"

I grinned.

"Only one way to find out."

And just like that, another lifetime customer.

The Legacy of TV Exposure

Being on TV didn't just boost business—it made me real to people.

They saw the passion. They saw the work.

And most importantly? They saw that I wasn't just another chef. I was different.

Since then, I've been on:

- Multiple TV segments

- Food Network competitions

- Online cooking shows

- Live interviews with national anchors

And every single time, it's the same feeling.

Excitement. Energy. Pride.

Because this? This is what I was meant to do.

Making Headlines: The Buzz Around Marley's

At this point, Marley's had already made its mark in print media and television. The stories, the interviews, the cameras—all of it was surreal but the buzz didn't stop there. The word kept spreading, and suddenly, we weren't just a local spot anymore. People were traveling just to try our wings, and before I knew it, Marley's was popping up in food blogs, radio mentions, and more news articles.

300 Flavors and Counting

One of the biggest moments came when Cat Country 107.3 called Marley's one of New Jersey's top wing spots. They didn't just mention us—they put the spotlight on what makes us different: 300+ wing flavors that range from Blueberry BBQ to Almond Joy, from Apricot BBQ Lime to Caramel Apple and Captain Crunch.

People weren't just showing up—they were planning their orders before they even got here. I remember reading about a guy who researched our menu, picked out his flavors, and drove an hour just to try the Captain Crunch wings, and when he left? He said it was worth every mile.

"Marley's Gotham Grill, located at 169 Main Street, is an award-winning restaurant offering endless flavors, including Blueberry BBQ, Almond Joy, Apricot, BBQ Lime, Caramel Apple and Spice, and Captain Crunch."— Cat Country 107.3

For me, it was never just about the food—it was about the experience. If people were making road trips just for our wings, we had to make sure they got something they couldn't find anywhere else.

A Bucket List Moment: Winning on Food Network

I've always believed in pushing the limits, not just with flavors but in everything I do. So when the chance came to compete on Food Network's "Cooks vs. Cons," I had to take it.

For those who don't know the show, it's a high-stakes cooking competition where professional chefs go head-to-head with home cooks, while judges try to figure out who's who. Hosted by Iron Chef Geoffrey Zakarian, the show put me up against a pro chef and two home cooks, with $10,000 on the line.

The first round? Pappardelle pasta with corn pesto. Not exactly in my wheelhouse, but I made it work. Then came the curveball: we had to use candy in the second round. I went all out with a scallops brûlée, blood orange gastrique, and a candy necklace shaved over the top like Parmesan.

That's when the judges started putting the pieces together—turns out my knife skills and the simple act of adding salt to the pasta water gave me away as the professional but in the end, the only thing that mattered was the taste, and my dish took the win.

Taking home that $10,000 grand prize was one of the most incredible moments of my career, and the first thing I did? Put the money toward my daughter's education and a much-needed family vacation.

"Bruno Pascale took home the grand prize of $10,000 on Food Network's newest show 'Cooks vs. Cons.'"— NJ.com

The whole experience was unreal. Competing, winning, being recognized on a national level—it was a bucket list moment but more than that, it proved that hard work, creativity, and a little bit of madness can take you places.

CHAPTER 4

Taking the Wings on the Road The Food Truck Expansion

After the restaurant took off and word spread about my wings, I started thinking about what was next. People were coming from hours away just to get a taste of Marley's. Some even made road trips just to eat here. That's when I realized something—why make them come to me when I could bring the wings to them?

I had always loved the idea of a food truck. There was something exciting about it—taking your best food and hitting the road, meeting new people, setting up at festivals, and giving folks a taste of something they wouldn't forget. I saw the potential, but it wasn't until COVID hit in 2020 that I actually pulled the trigger.

Not because we were struggling—far from it. We were doing great during the pandemic, thanks to a killer takeout business. The restaurant was booming, even when others were shutting their doors. So instead of sitting back and waiting, I thought, What's the next move?

A second restaurant? Maybe but that came with leases, overhead, and staff hiring nightmares. A food truck, though? That was freedom. That was mobility. That was Marley's hitting the road.

The First Food Truck – Marley's Wings & Things on Wheels

I didn't just throw a fryer in a van and call it a day. If I was going to do this, I was going to do it right. I got a custom-built 29-foot food truck, fully decked out with the equipment I needed to make wings at scale.

This thing was a beast. It had everything—

- A commercial-grade fryer setup to handle volume
- Plenty of storage for sauces, toppings, and dry goods
- A smash burger station for a little variety
- The speed and efficiency to keep up with long lines at festivals

We started building the truck in 2020 and launched it in 2021. And just like that, Marley's wasn't just a restaurant—it was a **traveling wing empire.**

Bringing Wings to the Masses

The first year with the food truck was nonstop. We hit up:

- Music festivals
- Farms and fall fairs
- Rutgers football games
- Brewery events
- Food truck festivals with thousands of people

We never parked it on the street—we went where the big crowds were. If an event didn't have at least 2,000-3,000 people, we weren't wasting our time.

And people showed up for us. Every event, the longest line was always at Marley's truck. Customers already knew the food, the reputation, the flavors. Even if they had to wait, they weren't leaving without their wings.

The Second Food Truck – Marley's Craving Cuban & Things

After the first truck took off, I saw another opportunity. One truck was great, but what if we could double our presence at events and give people a different experience?

That's when I had an idea—Why not do something different?

I've always loved Cuban food. Cuban sandwiches, Cuban steak with cilantro cream sauce, empanadas, yuca fries—I could eat that all day. So, I decided to build a second truck dedicated to Cuban cuisine.

The Inspiration Behind the Cuban Truck:

I won't lie, the movie Chef (2014) had something to do with it. That whole vibe of running a Cuban sandwich truck across the country? That hit home.

The 1,300-Mile Road Trip – A Food Truck Adventure

Bringing the Cuban truck to life was a journey—literally.

I had the truck custom-built in Miami, where some of the best Cuban food in the country comes from. Once it was finished, I flew to Miami, bought the truck, and drove it approximately 1,300 miles back to New Jersey.

That trip was an adventure. Every stop, people would come up to the truck and ask questions—

"What kind of food do you sell?"

"Where you headed?"

"You got food in there now?"

In South Carolina, a guy straight-up offered to buy food off the truck before we even had it fully set up. That's when I knew—this was going to be a hit.

By the time I got it to Jersey, I was exhausted—but ready to roll.

Inside the Trucks – The Setup & Strategy

A food truck isn't just a mobile kitchen—it's a high-speed operation.

Each of my trucks is set up for maximum efficiency:

The wing truck carries 25 of my best-selling wing flavors (instead of the 400+ flavors at the restaurant).

The wing truck also serves smash burgers, chicken sandwiches, cheesesteaks, onion rings, and funnel fries.

The Cuban truck specializes in:

Cuban sandwiches

Cuban steak sandwiches with cilantro cream sauce

Empanadas (beef & chicken)

Yuca fries and plantain chips

Cuban quesadillas

Both trucks are stocked and prepped before heading out, but if we ever run low, I have a Marley's van that delivers supplies so we never run out of food in the middle of an event. That's the level of preparation it takes to make sure nothing slows us down.

The Food Truck Business Strategy

A lot of people ask, "Why don't you just park the trucks somewhere full-time?" Simple—we're not a street food truck, we're an event food truck.

Every year, we lock in 85+ major events where we know there will be thousands of people.

- Music festivals? We're there.

- Big football games? Locked in.

- Breweries, farms, major city events? Absolutely.

We also do private events:

- Sweet 16 parties

- Corporate events

- Weddings, birthdays, and more

And the best part? Word of mouth keeps us fully booked. I don't even need to advertise—people call me. I get 10-15 event requests a day.

Running the Trucks – Crew, Logistics & Storage

Each truck runs with a three-person crew:

- One person at the window taking orders

- One person working the grill

- One person handling the fryer

Storage? No problem. Each truck can hold enough supplies to serve 1,000 people, and if we ever need extra, I have a Marley's van that delivers fresh stock.

Food Truck Fame – Viral Moments & Media Buzz

The food trucks weren't just making money—they were making headlines.

- North Jersey news outlets featured Marley's food trucks

- An Instagram post went viral – 70,000+ views, 1,300 new followers

- NJ.com and other big sites covered us

We became a household name in New Jersey and Pennsylvania. If there was a food event, people expected Marley's to be there.

Marley – The Name Behind It All

People always ask, Who's Marley?

Marley was my dog and my best friend for 15 years. He was there from the beginning, watching as the restaurant grew. When I opened Marley's, I named it after him.

I always joked that if a customer had a complaint, they could take it up with my dog.

Marley passed away, but his legacy lives on in the brand. Now, my other dog, Calle (a German Shepherd), is holding things down but Marley? He'll always be part of the story.

CHAPTER 5

Beyond the Kitchen – Passions, and Personal Life

There's a common misconception that when you own a business, it becomes your entire life, and while Marley's has been a major part of my journey, there's a lot more to me than just wings. I've always believed in the importance of passions that stretch beyond work—hobbies that keep you grounded, interests that keep you learning, and, most importantly, family that keeps you centered.

From collecting antiques that transport me back in time to pushing myself in the gym, these pursuits aren't just ways to unwind—they're extensions of who I am, and at the heart of it all is my family, the foundation that keeps everything in balance. Whether it's building memories with my wife and daughters or giving back to the community that has given me so much, these are the things that make life meaningful.

This chapter dives into the side of my life that people don't always see—the passions, the personal moments, and the things that keep me inspired beyond the kitchen.

Collecting Antiques: A Journey Through Time

Beyond the culinary and acting worlds, I have a deep appreciation for history, which manifests in my passion for collecting antiques. My home features a dedicated room filled with treasures from bygone eras:

- 1970s and 1980s Memorabilia: Items like vintage cereal boxes featuring Michael Jordan and classic kitchen gadgets evoke nostalgia and celebrate iconic moments in pop culture.

- Vintage Electronics and Appliances: From early food processors of the 1980s to a 1950s turkey roaster, these pieces represent the evolution of household technology.

- Literature and Media: A collection of "Mad" magazines and classic vinyl records offers a glimpse into the entertainment landscape of previous decades.

- Collectibles: Coins, baseball memorabilia, and other artifacts round out the collection, each item with its own story and significance.

This hobby allows me to preserve pieces of history, offering a tangible connection to the past and a respite from the fast-paced demands of entrepreneurship.

Gym & Weightlifting

Another passion of mine has always been fitness. I love hitting the gym and lifting weights—not just for physical health but as a way to clear my mind. The discipline of weightlifting reminds me a lot of running a restaurant or being on set—consistency, effort, and pushing yourself beyond limits. No matter how busy life gets, I always make time to train, whether it's at home or on the road.

Family and Personal Life

Family has always been at the core of my journey, shaping who I am and grounding me in what truly matters. In 2009, I married my wife, a compassionate and dedicated nurse practitioner. Her unwavering support, kindness, and strength have been a constant source of inspiration, especially as we navigated the challenges of building a life together. Through every chapter—whether it was growing Marley's, pursuing acting, or giving back to the community—she has stood by my side, offering encouragement and balance. Our partnership is built on mutual respect, love, and an understanding that no matter how busy life gets, family comes first.

Our greatest blessing came in the form of our two daughters, both of whom we adopted at birth. Adoption wasn't just a decision for us—it was a calling. From the moment we held them in our arms, they were ours in every way that mattered. The fact that they are biological sisters only deepened the bond between them and strengthened the love within our home.

Our first daughter, born in 2011, has brought endless joy and energy into our lives. At 13 years old, she continues to amaze us with her curiosity, kindness, and unwavering spirit. She has a way of lighting up a room, her enthusiasm infectious to everyone around her. Watching her grow, learn, and carve out her own path has been one of the greatest privileges of my life. She teaches me something new every day, reminding me of the importance of staying curious and embracing the excitement of life's possibilities.

In 2017, our family grew once more with the arrival of our second daughter. Now 7 years old, she is a bundle of creativity, laughter, and endless imagination. With her playful spirit and adventurous heart, she brings a dynamic energy to our home that keeps us all on our toes. Whether she's crafting new stories, creating art, or simply filling the house with her laughter, she has a way of making even the smallest moments feel magical. The bond she shares with her older sister is something truly special—a connection built on love, understanding, and the unshakable foundation of family.

Being a father to these two incredible girls has been the most rewarding experience of my life. Every milestone, every late-night conversation, every shared laugh reminds me that family isn't just about where you come from—it's about the love you build together.

Giving Back: Charity and Community Engagement

Community has always been at the heart of Marley's mission. We believe in the power of giving back and supporting those around us:

- **Annual Thanksgiving Outreach:** Deploying our food truck, we serve thousands of meals to hospitals, senior citizens, and individuals experiencing homelessness, ensuring everyone can enjoy a hearty meal during the holiday season.

Christmas Celebrations: Hosting events at Marley's, we invest in toys and create a festive atmosphere where children can meet Santa and choose a gift, fostering a sense of community and warmth during the holiday season. Seeing the smiles on kids' faces as they pick out a toy, some of whom may not have had a gift otherwise, is one of the most rewarding experiences of the year.

- Local Fundraisers & School Events: Marley's has always been about more than just wings—we support our local community through fundraisers, school sponsorships, and donation drives. Whether it's helping a local sports team, assisting families in need, or raising money for medical expenses, we step up whenever we can.

- First Responders & Healthcare Workers Support: With my wife being in the medical field, I've always had a deep respect for healthcare workers and first responders. During COVID, while many were struggling, Marley's provided meals for hospital staff, EMTs, police, and fire departments. It was our way of saying thank you to the people who put their lives on the line every day.

Giving back isn't just something we do—it's who we are. It's ingrained in Marley's culture, and as long as we're in business, we'll always find ways to support those who need it.

Acting: Another Newfound Passion

My foray into acting began unexpectedly. Encouraged by my wife to find a hobby—or maybe she just wanted me out of the house—I stumbled upon a casting call for the TV series "Billions." Without prior experience, I decided to give it a shot. I was selected for a background role in Season 4. The experience of being on set, observing the intricacies of production, and immersing myself in a new environment was exhilarating.

Eager to hone this newfound passion, I enrolled in a 30-week online acting course through John Casablancas. The training provided me with foundational skills and confidence, leading to roles in other productions:

- "Madam Secretary": Participated in a formal black-tie event scene, adding to my on-screen experience.

- "Evil Lives Here" (Season 7, Episode 1 – "It's All Judith"): Portrayed a corrections officer in this true crime series, delving into more serious subject matter.

- "On the Case with Paula Zahn" ("Tragedy in Visalia"): Took on the role of a perpetrator in a reenactment, challenging myself to explore complex characters.

- "President Zombie" (Upcoming Release): Embraced a role in this satirical comedy, showcasing my versatility and willingness to tackle diverse genres.

Balancing acting with my responsibilities at Marley's requires careful scheduling, but the creative fulfillment it brings makes it worthwhile. I've had the opportunity to stand alongside a few big names in the industry which I'll go in more depth in the next chapter.

CHAPTER 6

Stepping Onto the Big Screen: Bruno's Acting Journey

From the Kitchen to the Camera

Acting was never something I imagined myself doing. I was too busy running a restaurant, growing my business, and making sure every wing that left my kitchen was perfect but sometimes, life throws unexpected opportunities your way, and you either take them or let them pass.

My wife was the first to encourage me to find a hobby outside of work. She saw how much time I put into Marley's and wanted me to do something just for myself. That's when I stumbled across a casting call for Billions.

It wasn't planned—I was scrolling online one day when I saw an open call for background actors. Billions was one of the biggest shows on TV at the time, and I figured, Why not? I sent in my information, not expecting much. To my surprise, a few days later, I got an email: You're in. Report to set in New York. Just like that, I was on my way.

Walking onto that set for the first time was surreal. Seeing how everything worked behind the scenes, how actors delivered their lines, how directors called the shots—it was fascinating, and from that moment, I was hooked.

Building an Acting Portfolio

After Billions, I started actively seeking out new roles. I signed up for online casting calls, joined acting networks, and even completed a 30-week acting course with John Casablancas to sharpen my skills. Before I knew it, I had built up a solid acting résumé:

- Billions (Season 4, Episode 3) – My first role, the one that sparked my love for acting.

- Madam Secretary – A brief but memorable appearance in a black-tie scene.

- Evil Lives Here (Season 7, Episode 1 – "It's All Judith") – Played a corrections officer in a gritty true-crime reenactment.

- On the Case with Paula Zahn (Tragedy in Visalia) – Portrayed a perpetrator in this true crime documentary series.

- President Zombie (2025) – Took on a comedic role in this political satire zombie film.

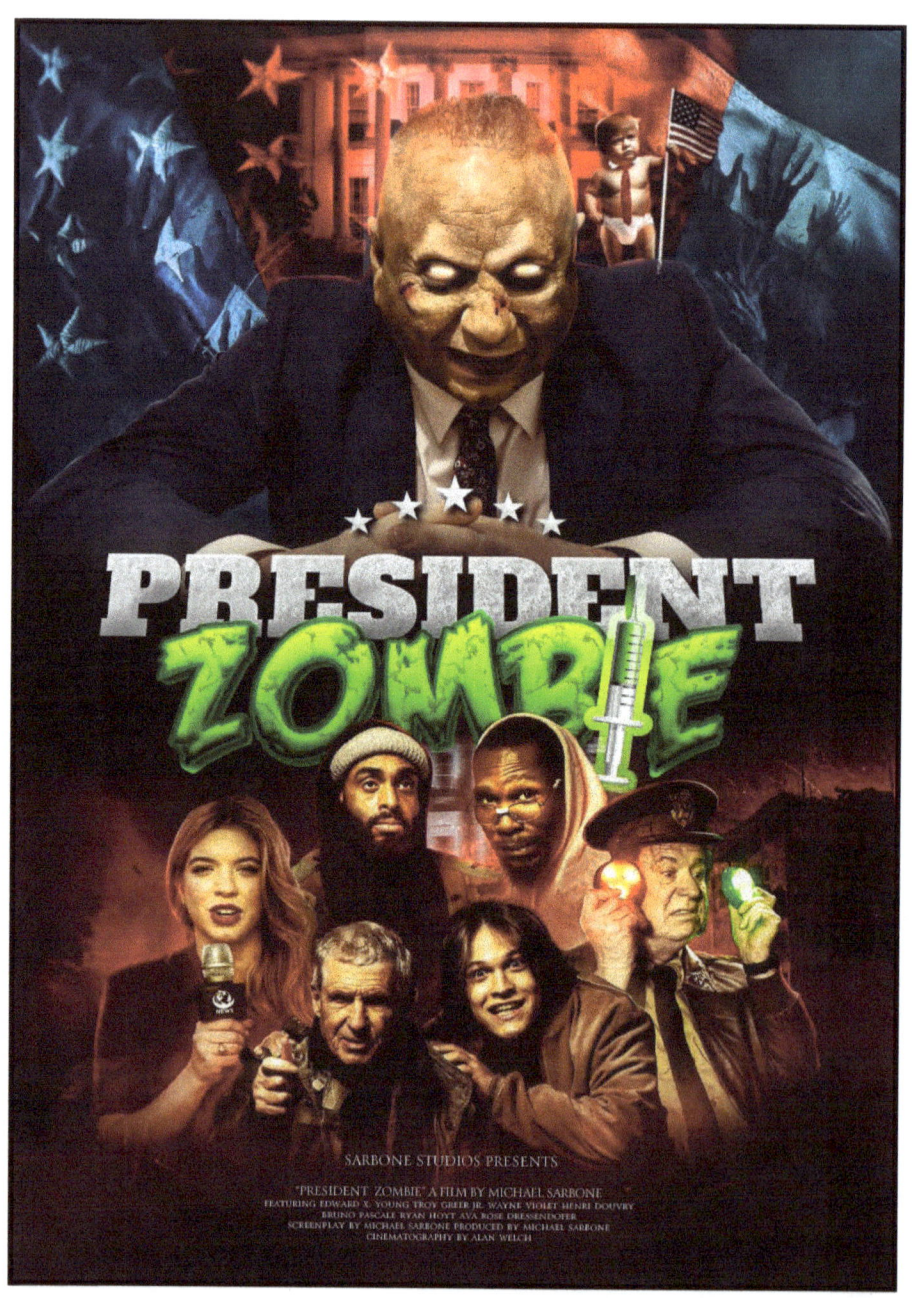

President Zombie Movie Poster

Over the years, I've participated in various independent films, including roles alongside industry legends like Paul Giamatti.

Acting is a world completely different from the restaurant business. In the kitchen, I control everything—the flavors, the timing, the experience. On set, I'm a small part of a much bigger machine. It's humbling, exciting, and completely unpredictable.

Another movie I've been in is The Black Card. Stepping into a law enforcement role was an exciting challenge, allowing me to bring intensity and realism to the character.

Meeting Industry Icons

One of the coolest parts of acting has been the people I've met along the way. Being on set and attending industry events has put me in the company of some incredible actors.

- Gianni Russo (The Godfather) – Met Gianni through a friend, and we ended up making it a special 'Godfather Night' at my restaurant. We put together an incredible four-course dinner, pairing each dish with wines from his personal winery.

- Paul Giamatti (Billions) – Shared a scene with him and got to watch a master at work.

- Rob Schneider (Deuce Bigalow, The Hot Chick) – Connected at an event and swapped stories about our industries.

- Doug Bradley (Hellraiser) – One of the most iconic horror actors of all time.

- Cast Members from Better Call Saul – Had the opportunity to interact with some of the talented people behind the show.

Every interaction has taught me something new about the industry. These guys have been in the game for decades, and just being around them has been an education in itself.

CHAPTER 7

Just Wing It

Looking Back: The Journey, The Hustle, The Grind

If there's one thing I've learned in this business, in life, really—it's that nothing happens unless you make it happen. You gotta put in the work, make the moves, take the risks. You gotta be all in or not at all, and if there's anything this book should tell you, it's that I was always all in. From slinging pizzas at 17, to running my own restaurants, to building my brand and taking my wings to the next level—it's been a journey, man. A crazy, exhausting, relentless, but absolutely worth it journey.

I didn't start with a roadmap. I didn't have some big investor backing me. I had an idea, a dream, and the drive to make it real, and let me tell you—people will doubt you. They'll tell you, "That's not gonna work," or "That's a bad idea." You know what I say? Screw that. Because if I had listened to the doubters, I'd still be working for someone else, clocking in and out, watching the days fly by, and that's just not me. I took the chance. I bet on myself, and here we are.

Chasing Passion Over Paychecks: Why You Gotta Love What You Do

I see it all the time—people stuck in jobs they hate, waking up every day, dragging themselves to work just for a paycheck. That's no way to live. If you've got something you love, something you're good at—go after it. Because you know what's worse than failing? Regret. Waking up one day thinking, "What if?" That's what eats at you.

Listen, not everything is gonna work out. You might fail but failure teaches you something. Every mistake I made, every bad investment, every wrong move—it all made me better. Smarter. Sharper. More determined. You just gotta keep swinging.

Family First: Priorities Moving Forward

At the end of the day, everything I do comes back to family. I've hustled hard so I can be there for my wife and daughters, support them, and make sure they have opportunities I never had. That's the real success—not money, not fame, but being there for the people who matter most.

I missed holidays. I missed gatherings. I made sacrifices because that's what this business demands but now? Now it's time to make up for that. Spend more time with family, travel, enjoy the moments that really count. Because if you're not living for that, then what's the point?

The Culinary Industry: Real Talk

This business? It's not for the weak. If you're thinking about getting into the food industry, let me lay it out for you straight:

- You will work holidays.

- You will miss family gatherings.

- You will work insane hours.

- You will be exhausted.

But if you survive it, if you grind through the tough times, the rewards are incredible. Because once you've built something, once you've made a name for yourself, you start calling the shots. Then you get to enjoy life.

When I was in culinary school, the dean told us straight up:

"If you don't want to work 12-hour shifts, weekends, and holidays, then get the hell out now."

That stuck with me. Because it's real and I've seen too many young chefs walk into this world thinking they're gonna be rockstars overnight. It doesn't work like that.

Lessons in Entrepreneurship: The Highs, The Lows, and The Hard Truths

If you wanna be an entrepreneur, be ready to learn the hard way. Research everything. Know what you're getting into. Because people throw their life savings into businesses they don't understand, and then they wonder why they fail.

Biggest lesson I learned? LOCATION MATTERS.

I once had a spot right off the highway, thought it would kill it but guess what? One entrance. No U-turns. If people missed it, they weren't coming back. That one mistake? It cost me but that's how you learn. Next time? I knew better.

Another thing? Partners. If you're gonna go into business with someone, make damn sure they're as committed as you. You don't wanna be doing 100% of the work while they're doing 10%. That's how businesses fall apart.

Success isn't just about a great idea. It's about vision, determination, and straight-up grit. Look at Walt Disney—he had an idea, he made it happen. That's the mindset you need.

Building a Strong Team: The Backbone of Any Restaurant

Your team will make or break you. Simple as that. A bad team? Your reputation goes down the drain. Customers don't care if it was Nick or Joe who burned their burger—they see my name on the place, and that's who they blame.

When I hire? I don't care as much about school. I care about work ethic.

- Show up on time.

- Be committed.

- Take this career seriously.

I don't wanna hire someone who's here today, landscaping tomorrow. I need people all in.

And teaching? Man, I've taught at three culinary schools—Hudson County Community College, Middlesex County College, and Northampton Community College—and I still teach every single day in my kitchens. You gotta be a sponge. Learn from everyone. Stay ahead of trends. Be willing to grow. That's how you stay relevant.

Faith, Family, and Living By Your Motto

I was raised in an Italian Catholic family and my wife was raised Presbyterian. One of my daughters is going to do her Communion soon, the other's doing her Confirmation. Faith is a big part of my life. It's guided me through the struggles, helped me stay grounded through the chaos.

And if there's one thing I live by, one thing that sums up my whole journey—it's "Just wing it."

It's my motto, it's my tattoo, it's how I sign my books. Because sometimes, you can't overthink. You just gotta take the leap.

The Blox: The Entrepreneur Bootcamp That Changed My Perspective

A few years ago, I got selected for The Blox, an entrepreneur bootcamp in Kansas City. Only 60 people from around the world get picked. No prize money, just pure education on how to build your brand. That experience changed how I see business.

I remember stepping on that stage, no script, no plan. I just threw my book down and said: "F* it. Just wing it." And that's what I did. That's what I always do.

Because at the end of the day, that's how you win in life. You take the risk. You push forward! And you just wing it.

Recognitions and Awards

Building Marley's into a culinary landmark has been a journey filled with hard work, creativity, and an obsession with crafting wings that people don't just eat—but remember. From day one, I wasn't just slinging wings; I was on a mission to make each flavor stand out, to give people something they couldn't find anywhere else, and along the way, that mission started getting recognition.

Our first major win came in 2011 at the Pocono Wing-Off, where our Honey BBQ Wing took home first place. I still remember standing there, holding that trophy, realizing that people were starting to take notice. It wasn't just about making wings anymore—it was about making a name.

The following year, in 2012, we went back with a Garlic Parmesan Wing that blew the judges away. Another first-place trophy. That was the moment I knew this wasn't just luck. We had something special.

From there, Marley's became a media favorite. People were fascinated by the sheer number of flavors we offered—at the time, we had over 140, a number that only kept growing.

- November 2014 – Daily Record Feature: A full spread titled "140 Varieties of Wings" put Marley's in the spotlight, highlighting our commitment to pushing flavor boundaries.

- 2014 – Star-Ledger's "Winging It" Feature: This piece showcased how we weren't just another wing spot—we were innovating, experimenting, and redefining what a wing joint could be.

- NJ.com's "New Jersey's Best of the Best": Being named among the top in the state wasn't just an honor—it was validation that all the long nights, all the trial-and-error with sauces, all the crazy flavor combinations were worth it.

- 2011 – Lehigh Valley Live's "Wing Showdown": This competition gave us the chance to put our flavors up against some of the best in the region. Walking away with accolades and new fans was proof that we were on the right track.

- August 11, 2014 – Unflappable Feature: This deep dive into our journey covered everything from how we started to what made Marley's different from the rest.

- 2011 – Express Times Feature: One of the earliest mentions of Marley's in the press, this was a turning point in getting our name out there.

Every trophy, every headline, every feature—it wasn't just about the recognition. It was about showing people that Marley's was here to stay. Each of these milestones pushed me to keep going, to keep creating, and to make sure that when someone took a bite of a Marley's wing, they weren't just eating food. They were tasting something unforgettable.

Marley's Wings by the Dozen – 2024 Stats

Over the past year alone, Bruno sold **tens of thousands of wings** at Marley's Gotham Grill. Here's what flew off the trays the fastest:

Flavor	Dozens Sold	Wings (Dozens × 12)
Mild	6,661	79,932
Garlic Parm	6,096	73,152
Honey BBQ	5,686	68,232
Bang Bang	4,091	49,092
Hot	3,152	37,824
Total	**25,686**	**308,232 wings**

What's Next for Me? Future Goals & Retirement Dream

So what's next for me? Man, I tell you what—I wanna be under a palm tree somewhere tropical, drink in my hand, waves rolling in, just kicking back and soaking up life. I've worked my ass off, I've built something solid, and now, I wanna enjoy it but that doesn't mean I'm slowing down completely.

My biggest goal now? Inspiring others. Whether it's young chefs trying to make it in the culinary world or entrepreneurs figuring out their next move—I wanna be the guy who tells them "You CAN do it" and actually show them how. Because I've been there, I've made the mistakes, I've taken the hits, and I've kept moving forward.

And let's be real—this book ain't the last one. I've got another book coming—one that's just about the recipes. The wings, the burgers, the legendary flavors. I know people have been asking for it, and yeah, it's happening. So stay tuned.

See you in the next book.

The Recipes That Got Marley's Gotham Grill Kicking

These aren't your average wing sauces. This is the real stuff—straight from Marley's kitchen to yours. No fancy techniques, no unnecessary steps—just bold flavor, easy instructions, and ingredients you can find anywhere.

Whether you're cooking for yourself, feeding your family, or trying to impress some friends, these recipes are built to deliver. So grab your ingredients, fire up the stove, and let's get into it.

The Old Hag

This one's sticky, sweet, and has just enough bite.

- 2 cups honey

- 1 teaspoon Cajun seasoning (any store brand is fine)

- 1 tablespoon Old Bay seasoning

- 1 tablespoon butter

Instructions:

Combine all ingredients in a saucepan over medium heat. Stir until butter is melted and everything is well mixed.

Yields: Approximately 2 cups of sauce

Good For: About 2 dozen wings

Dragon Fire

Sweet. Spicy. Smoky. This one brings the heat.

- 2 cups orange juice
- 2½ cups honey
- 2 cups soy sauce
- 2 tablespoons sesame oil
- 2½ teaspoons chipotle powder
- 1 teaspoon ground ginger
- 2 teaspoons chopped fresh garlic
- 1 teaspoon crushed red pepper

Instructions:

Combine all ingredients in a pot and bring to a simmer. In a small bowl, mix 3 tablespoons of cornstarch with 3 tablespoons of water to make a slurry. Add the slurry to the sauce while simmering and stir until it thickens enough to coat the back of a spoon.

Yields: About 1.5 quarts

Good For: 3 to 4 dozen wings

Hillary's Hot & Wild

It's got attitude. A little sweet, a lot of heat.

- 1 cup Cholula hot sauce
- 1½ teaspoons ground ginger
- 1 tablespoon butter

Instructions:

Simmer all ingredients together until reduced to desired consistency.

Yields: About 1 cup of sauce

Caesar Wasn't Chicken

Bruno's Caesar wing toss—straight from Marley's.

- 2 cups Hellmann's mayo

- 1 tablespoon chopped garlic

- 1 tablespoon Worcestershire sauce (Liam Perrins)

- 2 ounces red wine vinegar

- 1 tablespoon lemon juice

- ½ cup grated Pecorino cheese

- ½ teaspoon black pepper

- ½ teaspoon kosher salt

Instructions:

Blend all ingredients until smooth. Adjust seasoning to taste.

Peanut Sauce

Sweet, nutty, and ready to be remixed.

- 1 cup creamy peanut butter (Skippy, Jif, or whatever you've got)
- 2½ cups maple syrup (or pancake syrup)
- ¾ cup soy sauce
- 3 tablespoons sesame oil
- ½ cup sweet chili sauce (store-bought is fine)
- 1 tablespoon sriracha
- 1 tablespoon lime juice

Instructions:

Put everything in a blender and mix until smooth.

Yields: About 1 quart

Variations:

Elvis Wing: Add sliced bananas and chopped bacon

Thai Peanut Wing: Add more sweet chili sauce to make it a Thai-style blend

Garlic Parm

A classic done the Marley's way.

- ½ cup melted butter
- 2 tablespoons chopped garlic
- ¼ cup grated Pecorino cheese
- Salt and pepper to taste

Instructions:

Cook chopped garlic in the melted butter for about 1 minute in a sauté pan. Add grated Pecorino, salt, and pepper. Toss your wings in it. Optional: Sprinkle extra cheese on top after tossing.

Yields: Enough for 1 to 2 dozen wings

Crack Chicken

This one's addictive. Sweet, spicy, and totally unique.

- 1 quart orange soda (Fanta)
- 1¼ cups Frank's RedHot
- 1¼ cups brown sugar
- ¼ cup melted butter
- ¼ cup soy sauce
- Zest of 1 medium orange
- 1 teaspoon crushed red pepper

Instructions:

Combine all ingredients in a pot and bring to a simmer. Mix 3 tablespoons cornstarch with 3 tablespoons water, stir into the simmering sauce to thicken.

Perfect! Here's the rest of the recipe section—formatted exactly how Bruno wants it, ready for the "Real Flavor, No Gimmicks" chapter. All in his voice, clear, casual, and cookbook-ready.

Pop Your Cherry

A funky crowd-favorite. Sweet cherry heat finished with a pop.

- 2 cups maraschino cherries (stems off)
- 2 cups cherry juice (from the same jar)
- 1 cup cherry liqueur (Bruno uses LaRue, but any brand works)
- 2 tablespoons red onions or shallots, finely diced

Instructions:

Add all ingredients to a sauce pot and simmer for 10–15 minutes. Puree everything in a blender until smooth. Toss your wings in the sauce. Finish by sprinkling with cherry-flavored Pop Rocks (Bruno's go-to is Pop Rocks brand).

Yields: About 1 quart of sauce

Cheese Sauce (Base for Taki & Dorito Wings)

Creamy, cheesy, and made to coat.

- 6 tablespoons butter
- 6 tablespoons flour
- 3½ cups milk
- 1 cup shredded cheddar cheese
- ⅓ cup grated Pecorino cheese
- 1 cup American or Monterey Jack cheese (or any cheese you like)
- ½ teaspoon white pepper
- 1 teaspoon kosher salt

Instructions:

In a sauce pot, melt the butter. Add flour and stir until it looks like wet sand (1–3 minutes). Slowly whisk in milk, keeping the heat low. Add cheeses, white pepper, and salt. Stir frequently until smooth and creamy (about 5–10 minutes). Done when it coats the back of a spoon.

Pro Tip! Piggyback Wing: Add chopped bacon to cheese sauce and toss your wings in it.

Taki Fuego Wings

A crunchy, spicy twist.

- Cheese Sauce (from above)
- Takis (Bruno uses Fuego flavor)
- Hot sauce to taste (Bruno recommends 1 tbsp of Frank's RedHot)

Instructions:

Grind Takis into a fine powder using a blender or food processor. Toss wings in cheese sauce mixed with hot sauce. Sprinkle with the ground Taki powder and serve.

Dorito God

Another crowd-pleaser for cheese lovers and snack fanatics.

Instructions:

Same as the Taki Fuego Wings, but instead of Takis, grind up Nacho Cheese Doritos and coat the sauced wings with that.

Homemade BBQ Sauce

Sweet, smoky, tangy—this one's a staple.

- 3 tablespoons chopped garlic
- ¼ cup olive oil blend
  (i.e., 10% olive oil blended with other oil helps prevent burning.)
- 2 cups light brown sugar
- 2 cups apple cider vinegar
- ½ cup molasses
- 2 teaspoons dry mustard
- 2 tablespoons Worcestershire sauce
- 1 teaspoon smoked paprika
- ¼ teaspoon kosher salt
- ¼ teaspoon black pepper
- 4 cups Heinz ketchup

Instructions:

Sauté garlic in olive oil until lightly browned. Add brown sugar and stir until it starts to melt. Add vinegar and stir constantly (sugar may crystallize, just keep stirring until it dissolves). Stir in ketchup, molasses, mustard, Worcestershire, paprika, salt, and pepper. Simmer on low for 10–15 minutes until it thickens up.

Variations:

- **Honey BBQ:** Mix in a couple tablespoons of honey.
- **Hot BBQ:** Add Frank's RedHot to taste.

Bang Bang Sauce

Ka-pow! Just as the heat is smacking your taste buds, the soothing honey and cooling mayo come to the rescue, tamping down the spice—until that next bite, when the sensations repeat themselves. This sauce whips up in a snap. It's great on hot wings, but also try it on fried calamari, roasted tofu, or shrimp.

- 1 cup mayonnaise
- 1 cup Thai sweet chili sauce
- ¾ cup Sriracha hot sauce
- 2 tablespoons honey

Instructions:

Combine the mayonnaise, chili sauce, hot sauce, and honey in a small bowl. Whisk until well combined. Store any leftover sauce in an airtight container in the refrigerator for up to 5 days.

Yields: Makes 2 cups

Kung Foo Sauce – "A Bruce Lee Favorite"

No need for blue cheese with a sauce like this. Spicy and savory, it gives a different kind of kick to the taste buds. Serve with carrots and celery on the side.

- 1 cup aged balsamic vinegar
- 1 cup honey
- ½ cup soy sauce
- ½ cup sugar
- ½ teaspoon ground ginger
- 3 teaspoon cornstarch
- 1 tablespoon water

Instructions:

1. Combine the vinegar, honey, soy sauce, sugar, and ginger in a medium saucepan and bring to a simmer over low heat. Let simmer for 6 minutes.

2. In a small bowl, whisk together the cornstarch and water. Add the cornstarch mixture to the sauce, stir, and let simmer until the sauce thickens slightly (about 5 minutes) at low heat. Let cool slightly before tossing with wings.

Yields: Makes 2 cups

Fried Chicken Wings with Sauce Two Ways

Recipe from Marley's Gotham Grill, Hackettstown

Bruno Pascale has a passion for wings. There's no disputing that. Just visit his Marley's Gotham Grill in Hackettstown and take your time (you'll need it) reading through the 130-plus sauces he has available for his plump and crispy wings. Bring your friends and let everyone order a different flavor. You'll still need many return visits to get through them all to find your favorite.

Pascale offers here two of his personal favorites, and they're easy to make at home. So grab your ingredients and call friends over to watch the game. You'll need a moist towelette after you're finished licking your fingers. Pair with a quality beer (like the kind Pascale serves at his place) and you're ready for a bar night at home.

- Canola or soybean oil, for frying
- 2 cups all-purpose flour
- 1 cup plain breadcrumbs
- 1 tablespoon cayenne pepper
- 2 pounds chicken wings
- 2 cups Bang Bang Sauce (page 32) or Kung Foo Sauce (page 32)
- ½ cup chopped scallions, for garnish
- 3 tablespoons sesame seeds, for garnish (optional)

Makes: 4–6 servings

1. Fill a deep fryer or large cast-iron pot with 4 inches of oil and heat to 375°F. Line a large plate with paper towels.

2. Combine the flour, breadcrumbs, and cayenne in a mixing bowl. Mix well. Working in batches, lightly coat the wings in the flour mixture, shaking off any excess flour, and set on a platter.

3. Fry the wings in batches; don't crowd the pot. When the wings are done, they will turn golden brown and float to the surface; it takes 10 to 12 minutes. Remove from the oil and transfer to the towel-lined plate to drain while you start the next batch.

4. Let the hot wings rest for 1 minute, then toss with the sauce. Serve with a garnish of fresh scallions. Sesame seeds are good with the Kung Foo Sauce, if desired.